A Cry for Relief

A Crooked Tree Is Still a Tree

DAVID A. WHEELER

ISBN 978-1-64258-235-2 (paperback)
ISBN 978-1-64258-236-9 (digital)

Christian Faith Publishing, Inc.
832 Park Avenue
Meadville, PA 16335
www.christianfaithpublishing.com

Unless stated otherwise, all scripture references are taken from the Holy Bible, New International Version, NIV copyright 1973, 1978, 1984, 2011 by Biblica Inc. Used by permission. All rights reserved worldwide.

In consideration of the privacy of the medical professionals involved in David's story, names have been changed or deleted to protect their privacy. Medications, medical advice, or suggestions that were given to David during his surgeries and wellness treatments are in no way indicative procedures for anyone reading his story and should not be regarded as such.

Printed in the United States of America

10 Min Chips

Contents

Editor's Note 7

Foreword 9

Preface 11

Acknowledgments 15

Chapter 1

The Worst of Days and the Worst of Days! 17

Constant Pain, Doctors, Surgeries, Disappointments,
and Depression 17

Dawning of a Great Truth 20

Because of My Faith 23

Gleaning² Chapter 1 for Training in Love 23

The Suffering of God 24

For Discussion 25

Chapter 2

Events That Crush the Human Spirit 27

Advice from Experience 29

My Search for the Promises of God 31

Gleaning Chapter 2 for Training in Love 33

Praise to the God of All Comfort 34

For Discussion 35

Chapter 3

"A Friend Loves at All Times" (Proverbs 17:17a) 39

Some People Find It Hard to Make Visits 42

People Who Need People Are the Luckiest People
in the World 44

Gleaning Chapter 3 for Training in Love 46

Visitor's Etiquette 47

For Discussion 48

What did I do? Why God Angry at me?

Job

Steps

Jn 5 - lame man

Do what get well? →

Friend

Job

Not

Why

Prayer will often words

Chapter 4

A Word Fitly Spoken Is Like Apples of Gold in Settings
of Silver (Proverbs 25:11)...49
Gleaning Chapter 4 for Training in Love.........................53
Encouraging Words..54
For Discussion 55

Chapter 5

Yes, a "Cry for Relief" Is Heard, and the Power of God
Is Behind the Answer! 57
The Healing Power of Music..62
The Transforming Power of Prayer 66
Gleaning Chapter 5 for Training in Love.........................68
The Gifts of Art and Music..68
The Transforming Power of Prayer 70
Lord, Teach Us to Pray (Luke 11:1) 70
For Discussion 71

Chapter 6

The Road from 2007 73
Gleaning Chapter 6 for Training in Love.........................74
Remember the Caregiver...75
For Discussion 76

Chapter 7

Seeing the Holy Spirit and Walking Around the
Borders of Misunderstanding through the Gates of Grace......77
The Holy Spirit Intercedes for God's People....................78
Grace 80
Gleaning Chapter 7 for Training in Love.........................84
Grace: More Than We Deserve, Greater Than We
Imagine: An Interview with Max Lucado[15] 85
For Discussion 88

Appendix A: A Perspective from David's Wife, Carolyn,
        the Caregiver 89
Appendix B: David's Additional Thoughts on Depression 93
Appendix C: Suggested Readings...95
Endnotes 97

Editor's Note

The word *gleaning* is an ancient word, but it can give us valuable insights into the compassionate heart of God. He told the Israelites,

> When you reap the harvest of your land, do not reap to the very edges of your field or gather the gleanings of your harvest. Leave them for the poor and for the foreigner residing among you. I am the LORD your God. (Leviticus 23:22)

In the Old Testament book of Ruth, we see that Ruth's opportunity to glean from the fields of Boaz helped her to survive when she was at a very low point in her life.

> At mealtime Boaz said to her, "Come over here. Have some bread and dip it in the wine vinegar." When she sat down with the harvesters, he offered her some roasted grain. She ate all she wanted and had some left over. As she got up to glean, Boaz gave orders to his men, "Let her gather among the sheaves and don't reprimand her. Even pull out some stalks for her from the bundles and leave them for her to pick up, and don't rebuke her."
> So Ruth gleaned in the field until evening. Then she threshed the barley she had gathered, and it amounted to about an ephah. She carried it back to town, and her mother-in-law saw how much she had gathered. Ruth also brought out

and gave her what she had left over after she had eaten enough. (Ruth 2:14–17)

David Wheeler's story, *A Cry for Relief,* has the substance of words that can feed the soul who may be suffering. At the end of each chapter, you will find the opportunity to sift through his words to glean the depth of commitment that can be valuable in equipping each of us to be caregivers, a field guide for training in love, because there can never be enough equipped caregivers.

Sandra Mackey

Foreword

Everyone should have a friend like David Wheeler! He is a walking cup-half-full kind of guy, a modern-day Barnabas. I met David many years ago and was always impressed by how he seemed to know exactly what to say to people who were suffering and how to help the hurting. What I didn't know was his own story. After learning more about his decades-long battle with extreme illness, I wanted to know, "How are you so happy, hopeful, and helpful?" This book shares David's amazing story, including the gut-wrenching struggles that blessed him with wisdom and the practical steps to help when others hurt. Is this book for you?

- This book is for you if you are struggling with illness and suffering right now and feel like throwing in the towel.
- This book is for you if you want to reach out to someone who is in the trenches of long-term suffering but you are not sure what to say or how to help.
- This book is for you if you wish there were a resource you could give to others to equip them to help those who are hurting.

I wholeheartedly recommend this book not only to each person facing hardships, but also to all who want to care for and serve the suffering well.

Love first,

Don McLaughlin
Pulpit minister, North Atlanta Church of Christ

David Wheeler is one of those people who should be listened to on almost any subject. He is a wise and godly man. When it comes to the issue of facing pain, suffering, and obstacles that should never be in anyone's life, he should be listened to with even more care. He has been there. He has fought the good fight, and he has not only kept the faith but has also deepened, modeled, and challenged others of us to see how faith works in the tough times. We can only pray to do so well in our own struggles!

Rubel Shelly
Professor of Philosophy and Religion
Lipscomb University, Nashville, Tennessee

Preface

So many people, as well as friends and acquaintances who have also experienced extremely hard and difficult events in their lives, have encouraged me to write this book about how I have coped and am coping with my disability. I have read several books on how things ought to be in one's life following tragic events. But I have read none written by someone in the grasp of terrible fear and anxiety who told how things really are. I decided to write this book to try to tell you, the reader, how things actually were in my life while dealing with terrible back injuries.

I don't know what my reaction should have been in the beginning. I only know that I have survived to this present time. Perhaps I should try to gain spiritual perfection, but perfection has not been achieved by me up to this point, and I doubt that it will ever be.

My pain is manageable. I developed osteoporosis, perhaps because of the large amounts of steroids injected over a long period. My spine has three compound fractures. Arthritis has settled in my spine because of all the spinal surgeries. I also inject a prescribed drug each day, which, with vitamin and mineral supplements, have apparently helped my bones to stabilize. I have not had another fracture since I started this regimen.

In 2008, Carolyn and I were members of a church in Buford, Georgia, where I was an elder functioning as a teacher and had a responsibility for the worship services. I was sixty-seven years old and enjoyed painting beautiful watercolor masterpieces.

My speaking engagements on *Dealing with Disabilities and Pain* have taken me to churches and universities. I have held private counseling sessions, fielded numerous phone calls, and led devotionals at businesses for employees.

Carolyn, my dear wife, is the love of my life, and she is the savior of my physical life on earth. She has spoken to women's groups, and from the reports I received, she did an outstanding job.

When you finish reading this book, my wish is that you will find some tools to give you ultimate hope and confident faith in whatever your outcome may be.

> I have told you these things, so that in me you may have peace. In this world you will have trouble. But take heart! I have overcome the world. (John 16:33)

Drawing by Sandra Mackey

September 2017—*suffering* is an ugly word, especially when it's an undisputable part of your own life. It can literally destroy you—mind, body, and spirit. It can control you and turn you into someone you have never been. A loving, spiritual-minded person can become a crooked human being: bitter, desolate, wretched, and hopeless but still a human being.

Suffering transforms our attitude about ourselves. Instead of being self-confident and outgoing, it can humble us to the point of wanting to die. It removes the blinders to our vulnerability. It makes us fragile and weak, and it can often bring out the worst in us.

A crooked tree is still a tree. Not every tree is tall and straight, nor is any person exempt from pain and suffering. A tornado can take a strong, straight tree and turn it into a pile of rubble with one gust. Just so, none of us expects to experience the pains of loss, disability, and suffering that may come without warning but, in a split second, change the course of the rest of our lives. Even the strongest and most godly of human beings can reach a breaking point when the tragic events of life crush their human spirit.

However, one of the lessons that I have learned through this experience is that God is not finished with me yet; I can find strength in my relationship with him and discover that I still have gifts to offer him.

When I first wrote this book, I had been in the ministry for thirty years. Now it has been more than fifty-five years. The book has already sold out from second and third printings. My pain doctor has requested the book for his patients. It is proving to be a practical tool for training and use in caregiving rather than a theory or simple narrative.

How can we continue to have hope in what appears to be a hopeless situation? We must remember that God blesses even the crooked tree with what it needs to continue living. *A Cry for Relief* will tell you my story. I hope it brings you some measure of comfort to know you are not alone in your suffering.

Acknowledgments

A Cry for Relief came about at the urging of my wife, children, and friends. I genuinely appreciate everyone who had a part in making this book a reality, friends who gave me the computer program and showed me the basics of computer technology. There were those who taught me to use the computer, and when some things came to me slowly, they carried on for me. I am so fortunate to have friends like those who not only wanted to help me but also wanted to get this book into the hands of people who need it! At that time, prior to the first publication in 1994, I truly believe that my family and friends thought this work would benefit the people who could take advantage of it.

I specifically acknowledge and appreciate the encouragement and endorsements given to me by those who were my champions in 1994, some of whom have already passed to their eternal rewards. I recognize them here as having been important to my well-being and survival through many days of illness and healing:

> Jesse C. Long, then president of Greater Atlanta
> Christian School, Norcross, Georgia
> Edgar Walton, then elder, Campus Church of
> Christ, Norcross, Georgia

Now, twenty-five years later, with over fourteen thousand copies of *A Cry for Relief* distributed, there is still a need and still friends who encourage me to publish it again.

My wife, Carolyn, is still my source of strength and love. Her love, encouragement, and constant care continue to make my life worth living. I am very thankful for her, my children, grandchildren, and great-grandchildren, whose love and support give me hope for our future generations.

To my friends, Jackie Bradford, Don McLaughlin, Rubel Shelly, and many other brothers and sisters in the faith who have steadfastly encouraged me to this day and have blessed my life with their unending support, thank you.

Sandra Mackey has been the editor for this latest revision. I express my grateful appreciation for her contributions and what she has done to make this edition beneficial as a tool to use for training in love. May the result only bring glory to God, our Father in heaven.

It would be remiss of me not to acknowledge the tender care by the physicians, surgeons, and medical professionals who cared for me over the years, those who were dedicated to the healing of my body and spirit, with the guidance of God, my Father in heaven.

Endocrinologists, urologists, pain management professionals, caregivers, family, friends, and counselors, thank you for your tender care and concern. My story is still for you and any who may benefit from it.

Contact information: David A. Wheeler
2540 Ballantrae Circle
Cumming, Georgia 30041
Email: davidwheeler2540@att.net
Phone: 404-786-1104
Cell: 404-786-1104

CHAPTER 1 "REFLECTION"

The Worst of Days and the Worst of Days!

33 yrs ago

On a beautiful winter's day, a personal tragedy came my way when I severely injured my back. The accident occurred on December 18, 1986. At that time, there was no way I could know that this seemingly insignificant accident would have such a catastrophic impact on the rest of my life and the life of my family. Surely, most people could pick up a postage machine and set it on the back of a van without being injured. I had been accustomed to lifting heavy objects all my life, but this time, it was going to cost me.

My wife, Carolyn, and I went to our wonderful friends' farm for a Christmas party on the evening after my back was first hurt. My pain just grew more severe. I lay back in a lounge chair at the holiday dinner, but I could not get any relief from the excruciating pain. We had to leave the party early.

Constant Pain, Doctors, Surgeries, Disappointments, and Depression

What was I to do now? Whom do you see for back problems? If I went to a back orthopedist, would he operate? We didn't know the world's best, and we might pick the wrong surgeon. Finally, someone suggested a chiropractor. I went to one for two and a half years.

- ORS
- Nauo Surgeon

17

He kept me on my feet, but he could not correct the problem. My condition just deteriorated to the point that I had to find a surgeon.

Yes, you guessed it, I selected the wrong doctor. My wife and I had great confidence in this doctor, but during the first surgery, while installing large metal appliances, the doctor destroyed certain nerves in my back that will never rejuvenate themselves. This surgery took place in 1989.

After the surgery, my condition grew worse. Eventually, the same surgeon had to take out the metal because the muscle in my left leg started atrophying and I began to fall. The strength had gone out of the leg. This was only the beginning; it went downhill from there.

I could do nothing during the days and nights but lie in a lounge chair or bed and take pain medication and go to therapy several times a week. On March 26, 1990, the same surgeon performed a third radical surgery. He installed what he said was the largest metal appliance perfected for the back. He had told my family that he was going to use rods in my back this time. But when he came out of the nine-hour surgery, he had installed thick large metal plates, extremely long screws, and huge bolts in my back. He had also cleaned up all the scar tissue from the two prior operations.

After a short time, all the newly inserted metal began to work itself loose, and the horrible pain returned. I was forced to return to the hospital and remain there for almost a month because of the pain, which was accompanied by great depression. The doctor called in a psychiatrist because of my emotional state. Finally, I felt that he had at least done something right by referring me to this doctor.

On January 7, 1991, the first surgeon told me that the bone had fused and that I had completely healed. I asked him how this could be since I was in so much pain that I was hardly able to stand, much less being able to walk. Not convinced of the doctor's conclusions, that very same day, I took the same x-rays to a general practitioner, and he had his radiologist read them. Her conclusion was that there was only one bit of calcium that had formed, and there was no healing apparent. I was completely blown apart by this news. When I gave this report back to the surgeon, he tried to say it was in my mind and that I needed to continue to take medication for my mental state, according to his office notes. I have since learned that a doctor can say whatever he wants to say if he states that it is his opinion. He is protected, regardless of whether it is the right opinion or not.

I then asked the surgeon to send me to another specialist, who said that my back was a mess. He and his staff would eventually perform the first of two more surgeries. Before he performed the first surgery, he sent me to the department in the hospital that would draw blood to give back to me if I needed a transfusion during the surgery. I have always been borderline anemic, and because of this, the hospital administered a drug that would help my body manufacture blood. Members of the campus church gave blood for me. I did not have to use their blood but was grateful that they had given it for me.

The reason that my doctor wanted to use my own blood was that he would be sure that there would be no HIV virus hiding in given blood that no one knew about. At this point in time, I was in horrible pain again, the kind of pain that I wished that I could have forgotten.

The first of the two surgeries was performed in May 1991. This surgery was accomplished by entering my back from the back and taking out all the metal and more scar tissue. These appliances had worked loose and had wallowed out vertebrae L4, L5, and S1. During this nine-hour operation, the surgeon and his staff performed another fusion.

For the second surgery, he and his staff entered my back through the stomach and intestine area. The doctor took bone out of my lower left leg and pelvis area to remake parts of three vertebrae. He also did fusion in the front area of the back as well.

After the last surgery, I contracted an infection that lasted for many months. I still have problems from it. After each major surgery, I had to have numerous tooth root canals because of infections, although I have really taken good care of my teeth. The doctors said that they could not say that there was a connection, but I really feel that there was.

My reason for being fairly detailed thus far is so each reader of this book can be informed as to my great frustration and my perplexing situation. A doctor told me that, back in the late twenties and thirties, a person who had serious surgery either got overwhelmingly better or died. He said, "Now, you are not overwhelmingly better, and you are not dead. You are somewhere in between." No comfort there!

Maybe, by my relating these events in my life as a Christian, preacher, song director, development officer, husband, father, grandfather, and friend to many, someone in similar circumstances can find some resources to help him or her through the dark valley of physical suffering.

> Have mercy upon me, O Jehovah; for I am withered away; O Jehovah, heal me; for my bones are troubled. My soul also is sore troubled: And thou, O Jehovah, how long? (Psalm 6:2–3)

I always thought that, because I was covered with the blood of Jesus and I considered myself a devoted servant, I would be insulated from circumstances in my life that I would not be able to tolerate in some way both mentally and physically.

So far, I have been able to survive, but I have had no control over the events that have come my way. How I have reacted to these circumstances, I guess, has been the result of the thought and habit patterns that I have practiced in my life through the years of service to our Great Father.

Dawning of a Great Truth

From this experience, I have truly had the dawning of a great truth: it does not matter how often a Christian walks in and out of a building with the name of our Lord over it, or how much one prays fervently, or how much one is a soul winner, or how much money one gives to our Lord, or how many widows and orphans one cares for, or is not a troublemaker among the saints, or sings with the spirit and understanding, or manifests the proper attitude.

I have realized that we are human beings living in a world where God allows all the illnesses of mankind to be the same problem to his people as to those who are not his people. What differs between Christian people and non-Christian people is the fact that, as Christians, we have all the resources that heaven must offer. The unending, abounding help is there for us when illness and problems that are common to all people come our way.

I found myself in just as much pain, being just as frustrated, spending just as much money, having just as many unknown answers about my situation as non-Christians have. Yes, I had much rage toward God. I have been so ashamed for questioning God's love for me. Oh yes, I asked repeatedly, "Why *me*?" What could I possibly have done to bring on God's wrath over and over?

You see, there were times, and still are, that I didn't know whether I would ever be able in my life to again publicly proclaim God's love, lead congregational singing in praises to him, be the financial provider for my wife and myself, or be actively involved in taking care of other people. You talk about having a bleak outlook on life at times!

Yes! I had it. To some degree, I can understand what Job was saying in chapter 7, verses 13–15, when he said,

> My bed will comfort me, My couch will ease my complaint. Then You scare me with dreams and terrify me with visions, so that my soul chooses strangling and death rather than my body.

Job felt abandoned by God. What frustration, fatigue of the mind, and terror-filled days, and especially nights, he must have endured! Job just didn't understand God's way with him. When I read further, I see Job with a humble and contrite spirit: Listen to Job in chapter 23, verses 1–9:

> Then Job replied: "Even today my complaint is bitter; his hand is heavy in spite of my groaning. If only I knew where to find him; if only I could

go to his dwelling! I would state my case before him and fill my mouth with arguments. I would find out what he would answer me, and consider what he would say. Would he oppose me with great power? No, he would not press charges against me. There an upright man could present his case before him, and I would be delivered forever from my judge. But if I go to the east, he is not there; if I go to the west, I do not find him. When he is at work in the north, I do not see him; when he turns to the south, I catch no glimpse of him."

And Job 13:15–18:

Though he slay me, yet will I hope in him; I will surely defend my ways to his face. Indeed, this will turn out for my deliverance, for no godless man would dare come before him! Listen carefully to my words; let your ears take in what I say. Now that I have prepared my case, I know I will be vindicated.

Right now, I feel as if the reader will want to put this book down and will not want to read on to the end because it is so depressing. However, I feel that only by being open and honest can you understand where I have been mentally and emotionally as I tried to cope with this overwhelming disaster as a Christian. I promise you will know what a blessing it is to claim God's blessings before the book ends.

For his anger lasts only a moment, but his favor lasts a lifetime; weeping may remain for a night, but rejoicing comes in the morning. (Psalm 30:5)

Because of My Faith

Atheist writer Susan Jacoby wrote in *The New York Times*, "When I see homeless people shivering in the wake of a deadly storm, when the news media brings me almost obscenely close to the raw grief of bereft parents, I do not have to ask, as all people of faith must, why an all-powerful, all-good God allows such things to happen." She is right, of course, at one level. If you don't believe in God at all, you don't struggle with the question of why life is so unjust. It just is—deal with it. Jacoby says that atheism makes you "free of what is known as the theodicy problem," not needing to "square [terrible] things" in this life "with an unseen overlord in the next."[1] But you also have none of the powerful comforts and joys that Christian belief can give you, either.

Gleaning[2] Chapter 1 for Training in Love

1. What is the situation or problem? Christians are not exempt from pain and suffering.
2. Why does it matter? This realization causes suffering Christians to turn away from God's healing power.
3. How do you engage in healthy conversations about it?

> It seems to me quite disastrous that the idea should have got about that Christianity is an other-worldly, unreal, idealistic kind of religion that suggests that if we are good we shall be happy. On the contrary, it is fiercely and even harshly realistic, insisting that there are certain eternal achievements that made even happiness look like trash. (Dorothy L. Sayers, *Creed or Chaos?*)

Can we accept the philosophical idea that nothing makes bad things happen, that they just happen? Some people cannot accept that idea. They insist that there must be a reason for bad luck. They

mind of God to figure all that out—

"let this cup pass ... not my will ..."

convince themselves that God is cruel or that they are being punished because they have made him angry. But why must there always be a reason for bad things happening? There are many rough edges to our universe.

When God, in the beginning, created the heavens and the earth, he set immutable laws into effect. Day and night; seasons and climates were begun by him. Things like gravity and weight or force of nature and angles of projection; chemistry, physics, and biology; animal, vegetable, and mineral, they all have parts to play in our universe. God made it all perfect in the beginning. He also meant for man and woman to be perfect. It might have remained so if he had not also given us free will. But then, where would be the honor and glory for him if we had no choice in our obedient love for or gifts to him?

Trying to make sense of this universe is like striking a match to see the sun! Rather, give thanks for the God who is our present comfort in times of pain and suffering.

The Suffering of God

God is sovereign over suffering, yet in teaching unique to the Christian faith among many religions, God also made himself vulnerable and subject to suffering (Philippians 2:5–8). The other side of the sovereignty of God is the suffering of God himself.

As Ronald Rutgers said, "Holding both of these together—as paradoxical as they seem at first . . . is crucial to grasping the unique Christian understanding of suffering. One of the main reasons that Christians insist that God can be trusted in the midst of suffering is because God Himself has firsthand experience of suffering."[3]

fallen world

Sin in World

For Discussion

1. Can we accept the philosophical idea that nothing makes bad things happen, that they just happen? — *broken world*
2. Is all suffering a result of an unwise choice we have made?
3. Must there always be a reason for bad things happening?
4. How can we reconcile the fact that we reap what we sow and the fact that God does not *make* bad things happen?
5. How did God suffer?

"allows"

Others may cause suffering

Scriptures

may or may not be "fault" it is — how do we deal with.

GOD

CHAPTER 2

Events That Crush the Human Spirit

Lowest Point

> For the word of God is alive and active. Sharper than any double-edged sword, it penetrates even to dividing soul and spirit, joints and marrow; it judges the thoughts and attitudes of the heart.
>
> —Hebrews 4:12

My thought processing was a mess! You see, I came from a tremendous loving and caring Christian home. To a large extent, the church in northwestern Georgia is what it is today because my father and mother were so fervent in their dedication to our Lord. They raised eight children in this atmosphere.

From as early as I can remember, my mother told everyone that I was going to be her preacher. When I was fifteen years old, I entered Alabama Christian High School, thinking that I would be better prepared by starting Bible courses early in life. Later, I went to Alabama Christian College, which is now Faulkner University, and Alabama Christian School of Religion, now known as Southern Christian University, in Montgomery, Alabama.

While in high school, I fell in love with the loveliest girl I had ever met. We have been married for sixty years. The wedding took place on March 26, 1957, in Montgomery. We have raised three children.

Our daughter, Tammie, married Adrian Freeman Jr., and they have given us two fine grandsons, one great-granddaughter, and two great-grandsons. They live in Long Creek, South Carolina.

With Anthony, our eldest son, and his wife, Lynette, we have three fine grandsons and a step-granddaughter living in Springdale, Arkansas.

Our youngest son, Phillip Wheeler, lives in Duluth, Georgia.

Carolyn and I have worked through the years with churches in Florida, Alabama, North Carolina, and Georgia. We also worked at Faulkner University and Greater Atlanta Christian Schools Inc. (GACS).

I write this brief life's history just to let you know that I have been involved with people whom I believed were spiritual giants in the faith. But for myself, I often feel that I have hidden my faith and that God hates me and that I surely have been one of the worst people who has ever been in the faith! What could I have possibly done to make God so angry with me?

I preached regularly on faith, unconditional love, and God's care, how he knows the number of hairs on our head and that he will not allow us to be tempted above what we are able to bear. I have offered my family on the altar of sacrifice. My labor and service to the Father have been 24 hours a day, 7 days a week, 365 days a year for most of my life!

What more could I have accomplished? Why, oh, why could God do this to me? You see, before a catastrophic event came my way, I knew all the answers. But now that I was in a circumstance that I could do absolutely nothing about, all I had were doubt and questions.

I write these things not to brag about how spiritually weak I was, but to let you know how low my spirits often were for long periods.

Please bear with me while I tell you more of my dilemma. You must realize that the first surgeon did not consult another back surgeon to help him to know absolutely what to do for me. There were insurance forms on top of forms that were complicated and had to be filled out repeatedly. The doctor finished filling out the forms, but he still had to sign many of them and send them in by certain deadlines.

Now, have you ever tried to get a busy surgeon or other doctors to fill out forms correctly in a short period? I was down in bed, and my wife was working fulltime outside the home. Yet we were the only two persons who could take care of this situation. The wrong forms were sent to be filled out on many occasions. Trying to find someone at the doctor's business office and in the insurance office who actually cared one way or another was seemingly impossible. Trying to receive disability funding was just about impossible! I had to retain an attorney, which was very costly. Reading multitudinous forms that the insurance people themselves did not understand, or they pretended they didn't, was frustrating. Papers that supposedly got lost in the mail several times just made no sense!

Advice from Experience

When you are well and need no assistance, everything usually runs smoothly, but when you are helpless, it is a completely different story. I have learned many things from my experiences with doctors and insurance companies. Take these for example:

1. Never, never have a conversation with an insurance person without getting in writing what is told to you. The only safeguard in dealing with insurance companies is to personally read very carefully all the papers and forms. I urge everyone to read the fine print in your policies.
2. Keep in mind a good attorney just in case you ever need one. You will find that this will prove most beneficial to you, but you may still come up on the short end of many things.

In October 1989, my eldest brother passed away. Then in May of 1990, my sweet mother passed away. A few months later, my dear aunt died. She was determined that I would speak at her funeral, but

I could not. In fact, I was unable to attend any of these heart-burdened memorials. What a horrible situation! They told me that those who had passed away would understand why I could not attend their funerals, and maybe *they* could understand, but *I* absolutely could *not* understand!

In August 1992, I contracted a severe infection. On one occasion, Carolyn had to rush back to Emory University to pick up some medication. She had to get from our house to the hospital twenty miles in Atlanta traffic in forty-five minutes for this lifesaving medicine, not knowing where the pharmacy was in that vast hospital complex.

Just as she hurried into the hospital, the best back surgeon in the world was walking down the hall, and he was kind enough to show her to the pharmacy. I discovered that frequently, great doctors are great men! Such caring, such dedication, and such skill in one man—for this I give God the glory!

As a side script, during all these months and years, Carolyn and I were constant in the stewardship of our money to the Lord and to the congregation where we worship.

Still, during this period of my life, I could not count my blessings. I really was trying to do this, but I could not appreciate my blessings. I felt completely deaf, dumb, and blind to all that I had to be thankful for in my life.

Someone told me, "Look around, you can always find someone who is worse off than you," but this had no bearing on my thinking. I felt sorrow for everyone and everything. I knew the statement was true, intellectually, but for someone to think it would help me to apply the statement to myself, well, it didn't help. I was not ready to hear it.

By this time, because of all the chemicals administered to me by the doctors, I was suffering from a severe chemical imbalance in my brain. Because of this, I was then put under the care of a psychiatrist, a man who had great compassion and a strong desire to help me handle all the pain. He truly assisted me with the proper prescription drugs to handle the chemical imbalance. He also counseled me through this devastating situation.

Yes, I felt that I needed to be very careful to be certain that I had found the right psychiatrist. Going to a psychiatrist was a very big step for me. You see, I was living in fear that he might tell me to do or that he would cause me to act contrary to God's Word, and I was heavily involved with the Word of God and constantly in prayer to the Father while seeing this doctor. I had made up my mind that I was not going to let him influence me to knowingly do something contrary to what I believed and practiced. But he helped me through it with respect for my faith.

As a side note, I would encourage others to seek professional help if they feel the need for it. Don't be afraid to do so because of stigma or fear of losing faith. Sometimes, these counselors can be a great help.

As I think back on things, my mind goes back to January 1991. At that time, my mind was in such a state of depression and despair that I knew I had to do something differently or I would surely die. My human spirit had been crushed. I tried to pull my thoughts together and finally remembered something that Karl Menninger said, "Attitudes are more important than facts."

My Search for the Promises of God

I determined that, whatever it took to get my attitude right, that I would do! I had to stop trying to fix the blame for my problems and get busy fixing the problems themselves. In my conversations with myself and prayer with the Father, I came to the conclusion and confessed that I did, in fact and for all times, believe that God revealed himself in his holy and divine word. I felt that I needed to study the scriptures again like I had never studied them before.

I called the Greater Atlanta Christian Book Store and asked them to send me a loose-leaf Bible workbook. I asked for a version that I was not at all familiar with, thinking my mind would look sharply into it. I also ordered that version on cassette tapes. In my personal search of the scripture, I wanted to find the promises of God for me and God's power that makes sure that the promises would be kept. For instance, the apostle Paul wrote,

> I pray that the eyes of your heart may be enlightened in order that you may know the hope to which he has called you, the riches of his glorious inheritance in the saints, and his incomparably great power for us who believe. That power is like the working of his mighty strength. (Ephesians 1:18, 19)

That's what I badly needed at this time in my life. So I made a pledge to myself that I would choose one book of the Bible to be read every day for seven days. At the end of the seventh day, I would outline the book with the promises of God and the power of God to fulfill his promises in my life.

> In the hope of eternal life, which God, who does not lie, promised before the beginning of time. (Titus 1:2)

It was, for me personally, at that time and place in my life, the most beneficial mental and spiritual exercise that I have ever accomplished. I started with the gospels of the New Testament. There were three passages that I constantly quoted to myself every day and, sometimes, many times a day.

They are the following:

> Brothers and sisters, I do not consider myself yet to have taken hold of it. But one thing I do: Forgetting what is behind and straining toward what is ahead, I press on toward the goal to win the prize for which God has called me heavenward in Christ Jesus. (Philippians 3:13, 14)

> I can do all this through him who gives me strength. (Philippians 4:13)

> This is the day the Lord has made. Let us rejoice
> and be glad in it. (Psalm 118:24)

Throughout this particular period of healing, I had to come to grips with the fact that God had not singled me out and does not enjoy beating me to death, both physically and spiritually. I finally realized that I was living in a world where terrifyingly bad things happen to human beings, with no regard as to whether they are Christian or not. I was also made aware through the study of the Bible that my being a Christian has the God of all things at my beck and call to make sure that I would survive, even if it meant that I would leave this world in death. There are many things worse than death. My ready and capable God is able to see that I can hang in there! Finally, I reaffirmed the truth that God holds the future and he has not revealed it to me. I thank God for this.

> Trust in the Lord with all your heart and lean not
> on your own understanding. (Proverbs 3:5)

Gleaning Chapter 2 for Training in Love

1. What is the situation or problem? Dealing with events that crush the human spirit.
2. Why does it matter? In depression and despondency, a person may be unable to find hope for the future or remember that God is still in control.
3. How do you engage in healthy conversations about it?
4. Can professional counseling be a gift from God?

Hurt and pain are guaranteed in this world. Jesus tells is that we will have trouble but that we can take heart because he has overcome the world (John 16:33). Through scripture, we can be comforted by knowing that God is faithful and is always looking over us. He truly cares and is our protector and comforter in times of need. Whatever the circumstance may be, we can use these comforting Bible verses to find a peace that passes understanding![4]

God promises to comfort us. It's in the Bible: "As a mother comforts her child, so will I comfort you" (Isaiah 66:13).

God's promises are something he always keeps. It's in the Bible: "I will not violate my covenant or alter what my lips have uttered" (Psalm 89:34).

The promises of God are yes and amen. It's in the Bible: "For no matter how many promises God has made, they are 'Yes' in Christ. And so through him the 'Amen' is spoken by us to the glory of God" (2 Corinthians 1:20).

Praise to the God of All Comfort

Praise be to the God and Father of our Lord Jesus Christ, the Father of compassion and the God of all comfort, who comforts us in all our troubles, so that we can comfort those in any trouble with the comfort we ourselves receive from God. For just as we share abundantly in the sufferings of Christ, so also our comfort abounds through Christ. If we are distressed, it is for your comfort and salvation; if we are comforted, it is for your comfort, which produces in you patient endurance of the same sufferings we suffer. And our hope for you is firm, because we know that just as you share in our sufferings, so also you share in our comfort. We do not want you to be uninformed, brothers and sisters, about the troubles we experienced in the province of Asia. We were under great pressure, far beyond our ability to endure, so that we despaired of life itself. Indeed, we felt we had received the sentence of death. *But this happened that we might not rely on ourselves but on God, who raises the dead. He has delivered us from such a deadly peril, and he will deliver us again. On him we have set our hope that he will continue to deliver us,* as you help us by your prayers. Then many will give thanks on our behalf for the gracious favor granted us in answer to the prayers of many. (2 Corinthians 1:3–11; emphasis added)

For Discussion

1. How do we know that God keeps his promises?
2. How did Paul experience suffering in his ministry? *icons*
3. How was he comforted?
4. Must we understand what a person is going through to offer them comfort? *Jesus knows*
5. What are some things we can do to comfort others who are suffering? Open discussion.

Psalm 31:5–24

Into your hands I commit my spirit;
deliver me, LORD, my faithful God.

I hate those who cling to worthless idols;
as for me, I trust in the LORD.

I will be glad and rejoice in your love,
for you saw my affliction
and knew the anguish of my soul.

You have not given me into
the hands of the enemy
but have set my feet in a spacious place.

Be merciful to me, LORD, for I am in distress;
my eyes grow weak with sorrow,
my soul and body with grief.

My life is consumed by anguish
and my years by groaning;
my strength fails because of my affliction,
and my bones grow weak.

Because of all my enemies,
I am the utter contempt of my neighbors
and an object of dread to my closest friends—
those who see me on the street flee from me.

I am forgotten as though I were dead;
I have become like broken pottery.

For I hear many whispering,

"Terror on every side!"
They conspire against me and
plot to take my life.
But I trust in you, LORD;
I say, "You are my God."
My times are in your hands;
deliver me from the hands of my enemies,
from those who pursue me.

Let your face shine on your servant;
save me in your unfailing love.

Let me not be put to shame, LORD,
for I have cried out to you;
but let the wicked be put to shame
and be silent in the realm of the dead.

Let their lying lips be silenced,
for with pride and contempt
they speak arrogantly against the righteous.

How abundant are the good things
that you have stored up for those who fear you,
that you bestow in the sight of all,
on those who take refuge in you.

In the shelter of your presence you hide them
from all human intrigues;
you keep them safe in your dwelling
from accusing tongues.

Praise be to the LORD,
for he showed me the wonders of his love
when I was in a city under siege.

In my alarm I said,

"I am cut off from your sight!"
Yet you heard my cry for mercy
when I called to you for help.

Love the LORD, all his faithful people!
The LORD preserves those who are true to him,
but the proud he pays back in full.

Be strong and take heart,
all you who hope in the LORD.

1:05 Minutes

(65 Minutes)

8

7 Chapters

Chapt   10 minute → Depression
         10 Minute
         10 Minute

Others

CHAPTER 3

"A Friend Loves at All Times" (Proverbs 17:17a)

Being so crushed in spirit as I was at that time, my friends provided me with strength to work hard at getting better! Strong, intimate relationships are very important. A man in the throes of despair should have the devotion of his friends.

> Anyone who withholds kindness from a friend
> forsakes the fear of the Almighty. (Job 6:14)

The next requirement for me at this point was to make sure that my relationships with my family and friends were even deeper and more sensitive than they had ever been. This catastrophe made me realize as never before that, when all is said and done, my family and my friends are where the lasting human blessings are found.

When you are lying in bed for months on end, material things lose their appeal. I could hardly do anything for myself. My own flesh and blood brothers and sisters and their families have been such blessings during this journey.

I concluded that, when your health is taken from you and you do not have anyone else to turn to, you need to have been living in a very intimate relationship with your family without any ulterior motives. This relationship should have been built over the years with your spouse and family out of pure love for one another. They are always there for you, and you are always there for them—just because that's the way is. It just comes naturally for them to be by your side, caring for you.

When I injured my back, I was working for Greater Atlanta Christian School and the Campus Church in Norcross, Georgia. These great institutions have been absolutely wonderful in their care for Carolyn and me. Jesse C. Long, then President of GACS, now deceased, spearheaded a drive from friends and the brethren in congregations where Carolyn and I worked over the years, to ask them to help with our needs. Each of the congregations responded with care and concern. They were wonderful!

If by chance you have not heard me say "Thank you," please let me say it again now. Thank you! Literally thousands of cards, notes, phone calls, and visits have come my way. I have always said that the fellowship of the church is the greatest on this earth, and this has proven to be the case as far as I am concerned. The Bible said it best, "A friend loves at all times" (Proverbs 17:17).

You may find this hard to believe, but in September 1991, Herschel Walker (not the football star) came to my house and asked me a very simple question. The question was, "Would you like to paint?" At this particular time in my life, I could not watch the news on television because it was so full of brutality, it added to my depression. I could not read very much because I had a problem concentrating. Herschel asked if I would like to paint today. I laughingly told him that, when I was in elementary school, I could not stay inside the drawn lines, and it just got worse and worse as I grew through the years. However, before he left that day, I had painted a par 3 golf hole in watercolor. The painting contained trees, water, sand bunkers, tall and short grass, sky, birds, and clouds.

Oh, how I miss playing golf! Brother Walker came to my house every week, unless he or I was ill or he was on vacation. Sometimes, he came twice a week to teach me how to paint and dream of things beautiful. Truly, painting lets the sunlight of your soul escape. Now I paint not only in watercolors but also in acrylics and oils.

There is a friend who sticks closer than a brother.
(Proverbs 18:24b)

Herschel taxied me to the hospital repeatedly and sat through surgeries with Carolyn. He drove me to lunch to get me out of the house so many times. Yes, he is a very dear friend!

There was another couple, Sid and Sue Tyndels, who brought me a bird feeder and a book about birds. When they brought these to me, my hospital bed was next to a large window in our den. The bird feeder was hung just outside the window. Several varieties of birds went every day to the feeder, and they just kept coming. I kept thinking about what our Father had said,

> Therefore I tell you, do not worry about your life, what you will eat or drink; or about your body, what you will wear. Is not life more than food, and the body more than clothes? Look at the birds of the air; they do not sow or reap or store away in barns, and yet your heavenly Father feeds them. Are you not much more valuable than they? Can any one of you by worrying add a single hour to your life?
>
> And why do you worry about clothes? See how the flowers of the field grow. They do not labor or spin. Yet I tell you that not even Solomon in all his splendor was dressed like one of these. If that is how God clothes the grass of the field, which is here today and tomorrow is thrown into the fire, will he not much more clothe you—you of little faith? So do not worry, saying, "What shall we eat?" or "What shall we drink?" or "What shall we wear?" For the pagans run after all these things, and your heavenly Father knows that you need them. (Matthew 6:25–32)

Yes, if God is taking care of them, he most certainly is taking care of me.

My mind is flooded with what people did to encourage me and what they continue to do for us. On one occasion, a dad took his little girls, Maren and Ragan O'Brien, to see me and to give me some peppermint and get-well cards. When they left, they had no idea how much encouragement they had given me. Then Ashley, another little friend, sent me several cards, and her mother told me that she prays for me every day. The children's classes at church sent me many cards repeatedly. And my little friend Lauren, her mother told me that she still prays for me every night at the evening meal. Jesus said,

> Let the little children come to me, and do not
> hinder them, for the kingdom of heaven belongs
> to such as these. (Matthew 19:14)

The hugs, handshakes, kisses, and special handmade things sent to me convinced me that I am actually a very special person. The sensation of the human touch means so much to me, and it continues to have a tremendous positive influence on my attitude. During most of the surgeries, there were at least forty or more family, friends, and fellow ministers sitting with Carolyn.

In the past, I had always worked hard at making house calls and hospital visits. It never dawned on me how much good was done. Yes, I realize that there are those who do not want anyone to go by to see them, but I think they are in the minority. Wonderful things started to happen when other human beings came and prayed with us or when total strangers came by and said that they were praying for me.

Some People Find It Hard to Make Visits

Another believe-it-or-not experience revolved around other special Christian friends, A. W. and Mary Anne Padgett, who went to the hospital and to our home on numerous occasions.

Let me tell you a little something about what it took for Mary Anne to make a visit. Mary Anne has been racked with crippling arthritis for several years. Among many other things that she has accomplished in this world is that she was a violinist in the Atlanta

Symphony. AW dresses her each day before he goes to work. She has a full calendar of Christian endeavors every day. Would you believe that they have also called me almost every Saturday night for years? This couple has not ever lost interest in me. Oh yes, if you are ever in attendance at a Georgia Tech football game, you will probably see them in the stands. It doesn't matter whether the game is here in Atlanta or not.

I was able to attend their fiftieth wedding anniversary a few weeks ago. You better believe that a person like Mary Anne, who has such determination, has made an impact on me greatly and continues to encourage me.

Lamar Harrison in Mobile, Alabama, told me to call him collect when I need to talk to someone. I have a standing invitation to fly down and spend some time with him at his expense. He comes up at the most helpful times and takes Carolyn and me out to dinner.

Dave Miller of Charlotte, North Carolina, calls me each week to see how we are doing. People from all over this great nation have called and told me that they are praying for me. Whole churches have had prayer on my behalf on a regular basis. Ladies' groups have taken time to send me cards of encouragement and inform me that they were in prayer for me. Prayer groups and Bible-study groups have told me that they were praying for me. Hundreds of prayers from Christian people have gone before the throne of God on behalf of Carolyn and me. God just had to hear and fulfill their fervent prayers.

I would like to encourage you to tell Christian friends about your trials and burdens. Please get your circumstances out in the open so godly people can pray for you. Don't keep them a secret. People will go to your aid if they only know what to do. Yes, it takes humility, fear, anxiety, and trust in people to tell them where you are hurting and that you need their help. I promise, when you get through hard times, you will be glad that you let your family and friends know what you needed.

People Who Need People Are the Luckiest People in the World

Yes, I have really been blessed by many, many visits. There are still times when I crave for someone to talk to about issues of my life. When visits are rare, I sometimes feel that I have been forgotten. That is when Carolyn tells me that brethren have not forgotten me; they just are not thinking about me at that moment. Brethren are overwhelmed with their lives and hassles living in Atlanta. They are struggling to work; taking care of their families is overpowering to many people. Some are getting an additional education in addition to their work and family duties. And remember that the traffic is usually horrendous! Yes, I really understand what she is saying, but one can read just so many books, write just so much in my book, write just so many speeches, write just so much class material, paint just so many paintings.

At times, I have been hungry for someone to talk with me. Continual silence is truly devastating! I don't think needing to see human beings has anything to do with one's self-image, self-esteem, or any other such factor. I remember a song that says, "People who need people are the luckiest people in the world." I am one of those people who need people. Do you think that I am the only person who feels like that? I believe God made man to need other people. Isn't that why he made Eve?

This is a point of interest to me. The church that makes house calls is naturally going to grow because people need people. Everywhere I go in society, people really don't want my name. They just want my Social Security number or my account number or my driver's license number or something else by which I am tagged.

When I go to the bank, the same one I have gone to for years, the tellers still ask for identification. They hardly look up. My face is no longer important, just my number and my transaction.

Could it be possible that some churches are running away from the average person by just wanting their attendance and their contribution? Frequently, congregations put no emphasis on who the soul is or how he can be a part of the church. Just think how uninteresting the Bible would be had God left out the names and actions of individuals! Just think what a church could do for this old world if it really put a Very Important Person sign on every member and visitor. The church that has the Spirit of Jesus in it is one that settles for nothing short of *visiting* when tragedy strikes, that *visits* the hospitals, nursing homes, housebound people, as well as making a *visit* when people have victories in their lives.

Yes, I really believe that there is a world of people who need other people. When we don't go look a person in his eyes when he is hurting, we personally miss so much, and the person who needs a visit misses it too.

Again, I know there are those who don't want to be visited in the hospital or when they are sick at home, but again, I feel that this type of person is in the minority. I have known people who asked for no visitors and then became upset because nobody came! The big question that I have is, if Christians did not have the many pressures of life on them, would they then take an interest in visiting those who need people? The saying that people basically do what they want to do may be right. God surely knows the answer to that, but I certainly don't know.

If you have taken time to read this book, please let me encourage each one to not only talk of our Lord, but also to walk his walk.

Satan has worked his lies on the Lord's body, hasn't he? It seems that most people feel like they don't have the gift to care about people. Even if the church is organized to make visiting a priority, that doesn't mean that everyone in the congregation who needs a visit is receiving one. Many churches are in gridlock when it comes to compassionate, responsive, sensitive, sympathetic, and understanding care for 100 percent of their membership! Truly, the lonely, hurting, depressed people are in a dark world. We should never allow our Christian light of love to go out.

Going through this bout with loneliness, I realize that people caring for one another is the greatest source of encouragement that one could receive. Through those visits, Jesus will be seen in us, and because of our caring, loving spirit, some will be moved to go to him. If only the members of the church of God would move on to the lowly, downtrodden, and lonely, the result would be a world changed. Then we would not be like the world, but we would have shown the world that there is truly a better way.

> A word fitly spoken is like apples of gold in settings of silver. (Proverbs 25:11, KJV)

> May the Lord make your love increase and overflow for each other and for everyone else, just as ours does for you. (1 Thessalonians 3:12)

> Offer hospitality to one another without grumbling." (1 Peter 4:9)

> How God anointed Jesus of Nazareth with the Holy Spirit and power, and how he went around doing good and healing all who were under the power of the devil, because God was with him. (Acts 10:38)

Gleaning Chapter 3 for Training in Love

1. What is the situation or problem? Helping the patient to realize the need for family and friends during a crisis.
2. Why does it matter? People really do need people.
3. How do you engage in healthy conversations about it?

One word of caution here. When you visit sick people, leave the patient smiling rather than trying to figure out why you came by in the first place. Here are some helpful hints on making a visit that I learned in my illness.

We who *visit* should be careful when visiting. We need to know if one cannot have visitors, does not desire visitors, whether he has a contagious illness, or if the hospital stay is brief for only a day or so.

Visitor's Etiquette

1. *Be alert.* Don't take it for granted that somebody else is going to see people who need and should have a visit.
2. *Be selective.* Pick out those who need a visit with prayer.
3. *Be dependable.* Set aside a couple of hours to visit every week. The same time each week is great because it will become a part of your weekly routine.
4. *Be thoughtful.* Give a little thought as to whom you are about to visit. Structure your visit for that individual. Pray about the visit. Be mindful of your words. Many people with cancer still don't like to hear that word.
5. *Be positive.* If you visit many who are sick in one day, don't bring the problems of prior visits to people you have visited to that individual you are visiting at the time. If that person asks about another's condition, then feel free to share the requested information, being careful not to betray any confidences or reveal anything that person may not wish revealed.
6. *Be sanitary.* Wash your hands thoroughly when going from patient to patient. Don't go visit someone if you are not feeling well; you don't want to give them new germs.
7. *Be nice.* Carry some *honey.* Oh, not really honey that bees make, although that is nature's most perfect food. But you know, something nice, warm, and sweet. A little pocket angel is one thing that is usually received well. Christian bookstores have many suggestions.
8. *Ask patients if they desire prayer.* Ask the patient if they would like to be a part of a prayer. It is one thing for you to tell someone that you are remembering them in prayer, but to pause and have an optimistic prayer on the spot to get the sick person through the day and through those long-dreaded nights is wonderful. Carefully think about what you are saying in the prayer, and don't say one that sounds like it is the usual prayer offered. Oh, how sweet were the prayers from children on my behalf. Only love is shown.

9. *Be aware.* Be very conscious about the amount of time you spend with a sick person. The bodily functions usually come on a regular basis because of the IVs given to the patient.

10. *Be careful of small talk.* Incessant chatter is not comforting! Please don't tell a person how he really looks since beauty is in the eyes of the beholder! Also, please don't tell them that they look good when they have had the very life stomped out of them in surgery. Be willing to just sit with the patient without conversation.

11. *Don't apologize for not coming sooner.* The patient probably can't handle your guilt and his too. The important thing is that you are there now.

12. *Don't worry.* Sometimes, people put off a visit because so much time has passed since the person became ill. Don't worry about it; that person probably needs a visit now in the worst way.

To conclude, *please* don't let the trivial, though urgent, things get in the way of making that visit.

For Discussion

1. What things get in the way of our taking opportunities to visit those who need encouragement?
2. How can we learn to be tactful in our care for another person?
3)
4)
5)

CHAPTER 4

A Word Fitly Spoken Is Like Apples of Gold in Settings of Silver (Proverbs 25:11)

The tongue can hurt, and the tongue can help! But some of the irresponsible statements that some people say to severely ill people can be quite the opposite of comforting.

Whatever comes to some people's minds comes out their mouths! I realize that some people like to shock the patient, thinking that they will get them out of their depression or make them feel thankful for the other blessings they have. However, if it is a chemical depression, words won't help much. The patient needs the proper medication.

I can hear people say, "Why, David, how could you write that statement?" I realize that people primarily have good intentions, and their motives are, for the most part, good. But please, permit me to give you a for-instance. I have known people who have told parents when they have lost a child in death that God needed the child to be in his rose garden. Would you not think that since God created that child in the first place that *he* has the power to create as many children in heaven as he would like?

Do you have the concept of our loving Father as being an ugly, nasty, uncaring, hateful, arrogant God? I have even heard of people telling a father who has lost his young wife and the mother of his children that God needed her worse than he did! Surely, one cannot

49

entertain the idea that God needed her more than those small children needed their mother!

I have never read anywhere in God's Holy Word that he would even have such a thought under the Christian dispensation. Oh yes, if he wanted to, he can do anything that he chooses to do. But in my opinion, I don't believe his nature would allow him to do this.

A Christian lady told me the other day that, while her mother, who had recently passed away, was lying beside them in a casket, someone told her that this facet of her life was over and she must go on with her life. Can you imagine how cruel this lady's words sounded in the name of meaning well?

Well-meaning people have made some thoughtless statements, innuendoes, and insinuations to me during a time when I was weak and vulnerable.

1. "Your accident will be for your own good." What they meant is that God has severely punished me for my own good and I should bear it like a man. I believe I was a pretty good man before my accident. Are they saying that losing my health, losing my income, losing most of my mobility, not being able to preach, teach, or lead singing are for my own good?

    I may be blind to what they mean, but I just cannot accept that God singled me out and said, "OK, Jesus, Holy Spirit, and angels, let's give it to David with full force so he will be made into our spiritual image." Would it not have been better to say "You are going through this situation to reward you with a depth of appreciation for people who are going through similar problems"?

2. Read this statement: "You will become the humblest person you could possibly be when all this is over." Do they mean that I needed this accident to become humble? Now, I thought I was kind of a humble person before this tragedy. That statement isn't spoken with arrogance. I realize that everyone needs more humility, but I was struggling for my very existence, and I needed a healthy faith in God. I

didn't need to be reminded of the great fear I already had. I feared that because I was not a better Christian, that God allowed this devastating accident and resulting illness to come my way.

I wonder if the person who makes this kind of statement can define the meaning of *humility*. It would have been better if they had said something like "I know that you are at the lowest position in your life, but do you think that this might have come upon you, not for humility's sake, but for greater service's sake?"

Now I watch how I say a prayer for God to please make me the humblest man that I can possibly be.

3. "You need to count your blessings!" Isn't that a flippant statement? Yes, I did and do need to count my blessings, but it was and is very hard to always do so. I tried time and time again to be so thankful for the health I had left to deal and live with, but sometimes I really had to fight bitterness and anger. I still fight this problem, and I still wonder why, at Carolyn's age, she is having to add me to her burdens. Why is she having to go through what she has had to go through at work? Why does she have to go to school at night to learn to use computers so that she will be able to get another position if her company is dissolved? She has worked so that we can keep our home.

Yes, we are no better or worse than anyone else, but after a lifetime in our Master's service, why has it had to come to this as far as *she* is concerned? We have always worked with churches that did not have money for retirement or funds for catastrophic medical insurance to take care of the preacher. That, within itself, remains a controversial subject among many churches, but at that time, I did not receive enough funds to take care of something like this. The churches and I always thought the Lord would provide. We forgot that he gave us a mind and judgment to take care of these matters. I am very thankful to the Lord for his care.

But godliness with contentment is great gain. For we brought nothing into the world, and we can take nothing out of it. But if we have food and clothing, we will be content with that. (1 Timothy 6:6–8)

Keep your lives free from the love of money and be content with what you have, because God has said, "Never will I leave you; never will I forsake you." (Hebrews 13:5)

4. "Everything is going to be all right." Yes, I really believe that everything is going to be all right in heaven. The only trouble with that is, I am not there yet! I am more than a little concerned about the here and now! I am praying that God will help me make choices now that will help me be a giver and not a receiver all the time.

Jesus Christ is the same yesterday and today and forever. (Hebrews 13:8)

5. "There are a lot of people who are in a worse health situation than you are in."
    This has been said to me many times at the wrong times. Yes, I feel that is very true, but that does not lessen my problems one bit. I have a tremendous empathy for all who have health problems. (There go those attitude blasters again.) I am currently receiving treatment at the Emory University Hospital Pain Center, and because of this, I can write some horrible stories where numerous patients are worse off than I am. I guess it is like closing the car door on my finger. I know that there are other people suffering, but at this point, I just cannot comprehend their plight. It is not that I feel sorrow for myself or that I have been or that

I am having a pity party; it's just the fact that I was unable to feel their hurt with my hurt.

6. "If you could recall the past years, would you still have elected to have surgery?" That question makes me sad because I did everything to keep from having back surgery. For me to have a ray of hope for a normal life, I had no choice. (By the way, the first surgeon told me that I would be back on the golf course in three months.) So even if I were able to recall the past years, I made the only decision I could have made at the time.

7. I could go on and on with stories like these. It is no wonder that we have reared a generation who mistakenly thinks that God is an ugly tyrant.

LORD, I know that people's lives are not their own; it is not for them to direct their steps. (Jeremiah 10:23)

Not long ago, I was asked by a tactless person if preachers still got hungry, implying that I am a failure now because of my injury. I think the question was asked in jest, but he didn't have a clue of what he thoughtlessly asked. By the way, they didn't give me anything to eat. I am trying to be tough-minded, but words like those shatter me to the core of my being. I ask myself, why would someone get their kicks by making fun of me? No doubt, he was just insensitive.

How sweet are your words to my taste, sweeter than honey to my mouth! (Psalm 119:103)

Gleaning Chapter 4 for Training in Love

1. What is the situation or problem? Measuring our words carefully so we do no harm.

2. Why does it matter? Thoughtful expressions of love and concern are important, especially to the patient's mental health.

3. How do you engage in healthy conversations about it?

Encouraging Words

Words are powerful tools. When a friend is discouraged or having a difficult time, the right words can clear their outlook and lift their spirits. Other times, there may be a person who does great work and deserves an encouraging note, and the right words from you will make all the difference.[5]

There is a children's book called *Alexander and the Terrible, Horrible, No Good, Very Bad Day*. Alexander wakes up with gum in his hair, his best friend has deserted him, there's no dessert in his lunch bag, and he's served lima beans for dinner.

Are there days when you can relate to Alexander—when you have a terrible, horrible, no-good, very bad day? Maybe you're feeling that way today.

Sometimes we wake up in the morning, and before our feet hit the floor, we know the day is careening downhill fast. Life pummels us with disappointments, challenges, and heartache, or maybe there's no obvious reason—our mood just shifts from lighthearted to heavy laden.

When I'm having a no-good, very-bad day, my first reaction is to push through and ignore my feelings. I don't want to feel bad, so I think, if I just keep moving, I'll shake it off. This works on occasion, but other times, it feels like moving through quicksand. I have no motivation or desire to do anything.

This is the time when I need some encouraging words and inspiration. I need some momentum to pull myself out of the doldrums and reframe my thoughts. As I replace negative thoughts with inspiring words and ideas, I find my feelings often follow.[6]

For Discussion

Tact: a keen sense of what to do or say in order to maintain good relations with others or avoid offense.[7]

1. How can a person develop a sense of tactfulness?
2. Why would you want to be tactful when you visit someone who is sick or who is depressed?
3. When you need encouraging words to lift yourself or someone else, just Google it! You will find good words to share because there is much to glean! How can we use the information we find on the internet?
4. Write down five more words that are synonyms for *tact*.

5.

Job 11:16-18

"This Too Shall Pass"

Lincoln Hawthorne

Music Prayer

CHAPTER 5

Yes, a "Cry for Relief" Is Heard, and the Power of God Is Behind the Answer!

You will surely forget your trouble,
recalling it only as waters gone by.
Life will be brighter than noonday,
and darkness will become like morning.
You will be secure, because there is hope;
you will look about you and
take your rest in safety.

—Job 11:16–18

Chronic pain is always the same, and at the same time, it is different for me. It goes up, down, sideways, upside down and crooked. It is never smooth sailing for me.

I realize that the statement *"This too shall pass"* is used so often, like the words "I love you," that it could lose its effectiveness, but they really have a depth of meaning to me. I knew that Solomon drew the conclusion in his book, Ecclesiastes, but I wondered where the statement originated.

I called the librarian at the Greater Atlanta Christian School Library. She sent me two documents that showed two men who were using the phrase and who were born and died about the same time. One was Abraham Lincoln, who used that phrase in a speech before the Civil War. This is what he said: "It is said an Eastern monarch once charged his wise men to invent him a sentence to be ever in view, and which should be true and appropriate in all times and situations. They presented him the words, 'And this, too, shall pass away.' How much it expresses! How chastening in the hour of pride! How consoling in the depths of afflictions!" This statement is from his speech to the Wisconsin State Agricultural Society, Milwaukee (September 30, 1859).

Nathaniel Hawthorne used the statement in his novel *The Marble Faun* (1860). He used it like this: "This greatest mortal consolation, which we derive from the transitoriness of all things—from the right of saying in every conjuncture, 'This Too Shall Pass Away.'"

To me, this statement is so very true and is ever on my mind, whether it pertains to the pain of the moment, day, month, or year. A Christian friend, Marilyn Long, once told Carolyn that nothing ever remains the same on this earth. Everything stays in a constant state of change.

When I finally realized that the *pain* is like life, when I fathomed the fact that *life* is a vapor that appears for a little time and then vanishes, I then understood that pain will vanish. "This too shall pass away."

> Now listen, you who say, "Today or tomorrow we will go to this or that city, spend a year there, carry on business and make money." Why, you do not even know what will happen tomorrow. What is your life? You are a mist that appears for a little while and then vanishes. (James 4:13–14)

> God has promised, "He *will wipe every tear from their eyes.* There will be *no more death or mourning or crying or pain,* for the old order of things has passed away." (Revelation 21:4)

God said He does not lie, *"in the hope of eternal life, which God, who does not lie, promised before the beginning of time."* (Titus 1:1)

However, as it is written: "What no eye has seen, what no ear has heard, and what no human mind has conceived—the things God has prepared for those who love him—these are the things God has revealed to us by his Spirit. (1 Corinthians 2:9–10)

People are very concerned about my health, and they ask me all the time how I am doing. I feel like they think, because I look great on the outside, I look that way on the inside. They also hope that God has healed me. I tell them I am "hanging in there."

A judge who was ruling on my disability said that I looked like a young fifty-two-year-old man. He could not see on the inside! I wondered how an old fifty-two-year-old looks. I was fifty-three at that time, and I wonder what he would say now that I am seventy-seven. I was truly thankful to be a young-looking person on the outside, but it didn't help my feelings on the inside.

It's true, God has not chosen to heal me. I don't know what the future holds, but George Bailey, a preacher in Dallas, Texas, once said in a sermon during a campaign for Christ in Mobile, Alabama, that he did not know what the future holds, but he knew who holds the future (*God*). I feel the same way about the future.

I still have some major problems to deal with. Recently, the doctor who has helped me so much with the chemical imbalance passed away at the age of forty-three. We were very close, and I wonder if I will find someone who will help me as much as he did. Here is another "unknown happening" with no conclusion, no rhyme or reason to me.

I am able to pass through times like these because of my faith. I could not and cannot deny the power of God and the power of his grace in my life. His providential care is ever abundant in my life.

For we do not have a high priest who is unable to empathize with our weaknesses, but we have one who has been tempted in every way, just as we are—yet he did not sin. Let us then approach God's throne of grace with confidence, *so that we may receive mercy and find grace to help us in our time of need.* (Hebrews 4:15–16)

I cannot bring myself to say that things are improving as far as my back is concerned, but I can say things are better than ever as far as my fellowship with the Father is concerned and the outlook for my spiritual welfare.

God, through the apostle Paul, said, "What, then, shall we say in response to these things? If God is for us, who can be against us? He who did not spare his own Son, but gave him up for us all—how will he not also, along with him, graciously give us all things? Who will bring any charge against those whom God has chosen? It is God who justifies. Who then is the one who condemns? No one. Christ Jesus who died—more than that, who was raised to life—is at the right hand of God and is also interceding for us. Who shall separate us from the love of Christ? Shall trouble or hardship or persecution or famine or nakedness or danger or sword? As it is written: "For your sake we face death all day long; we are considered as sheep to be slaughtered."

No, in all these things we are more than conquerors through him who loved us. For I am convinced that neither death nor life, neither angels nor demons, neither the present nor the future, nor any powers, neither height nor depth, nor anything else in all creation, will be able to

separate us from the love of God that is in Christ
Jesus our Lord. (Romans 8:31–39)

I accept and believe that promise with all my heart!

I feel that my lot in life is to meet the challenge of setting the
proper example in dealing with this catastrophic situation in which I
find myself. Several anguish-laden people have told me of their plight
and informed me that, because they are dealing with their problem, I
can too. Then, there are those who say that I need to keep on keeping
on because I am an encouragement to them.

I have never been one to blow out the flame of hope. I have
always been one of the ones to light it and to keep it burning.

Katie Cassetty, who recently passed away, said that I meant
so much to her in helping her to deal with her fatal disease. Jerry
Shackelford, who is fighting a serious, debilitating illness, said that
I was a great inspiration to him personally and to so many in the
church. The list goes on and on from people who need some direction or tool that they can use to bear up against tremendous odds.

If you are in any situation in which you feel inadequate to handle it or you feel that your faith in God is so weak that it may die, or
you don't have any faith in God, please know that, as a child of God,
you can reaffirm your faith or become a person full of faith again.

If you cannot call God your Father, Jesus your Savior, and his
family as your family, please consider giving God a chance in your
life. There are Christian people all around you who are willing to
help. Some of them have experienced circumstances similar to yours.

Please remember that, in God's eyes, you are more valuable than
all the world. Hold this thought in your heart continually, and never
doubt that it is so. I think that this poem by Helen Steiner Rice really
speaks to our situation:

> If I can endure for this minute
> Whatever is happening to me,
> No matter how heavy my heart is
> Or how dark the moment may be—
> If I can but keep on believing

What I know in my heart to be true,
That darkness will fade with the morning
And that this will pass away, too—
Then nothing in life can defeat me
For as long as this knowledge remains
I can suffer whatever is happening
For I know God will break all the chains
That are binding me tight in the darkness
and trying to fill me with fear—
For there is no night without dawning
And I know that my morning is near.

The Healing Power of Music

You may remember that I stated earlier that it comforted me when I listened to some of the great music of the ages. One of the songs that help helped me most was a song on a cassette tape sung by the group Serenade, from Huntsville, Alabama, titled, "Broken Things." That wonderful song spoke to me. Other songs that have a tremendous bearing on me were "Great Is Thy Faithfulness," "Through It All," "The Long and Winding Road," and "Climb Every Mountain." "Zippidi do da, zippidi aye. My, oh my, what a wonderful day!"

And this one is especially comforting:

In Christ Alone

By Andrew Shawn Craig, Donald A. Koch

In Christ alone my hope is found
He is my light, my strength, my song
This Cornerstone, this solid ground
Firm through the fiercest drought and storm
What heights of love, what depths of peace

When fears are stilled, when strivings cease
My Comforter, my All in All
Here in the love of Christ I stand
In Christ alone, who took on flesh
Fullness of God in helpless babe
This gift of love and righteousness
Scorned by the ones He came to save
'Til on that cross as Jesus died
The wrath of God was satisfied
For every sin on Him was laid
Here in the death of Christ I live
There in the ground His body lay
Light of the world by darkness slain
Then bursting forth in glorious Day
Up from the grave He rose again
And as He stands in victory
Sin's curse has lost its grip on me
For I am His and He is mine
Bought with the precious blood of Christ
No guilt in life, no fear in death
This is the power of Christ in me
From life's first cry to final breath
Jesus commands my destiny
No power of hell, no scheme of man
Can ever pluck me from His hand
Till He returns or calls me home
Here in the power of Christ I'll stand.[8]

Then there is a great old song entitled "It Is No Secret What God Can Do." I first heard this song when it was sung at a schoolmate's funeral when I was in the fifth grade. I say that one can have better control over his emotions in a time of hurt if he will let beautiful music into his heart. You may not hurt any less, but you will be more fulfilled and quieted in your mind's turmoil so that you can rest and be relaxed.

Because He Lives

By Kristin Chenoweth

God sent His son, they called Him Jesus
He came to love, heal and forgive
He lived and died to buy my pardon
An empty grave is there to prove my savior lives
Because He lives, I can face tomorrow
Because He lives, all fear is gone
Because I know He holds the future
And life is worth the living, just because He lives
How sweet to hold a newborn baby
And feel the pride and joy He gives
But greater still the calm assurance
This child can face uncer-
tain day, because He lives
Because He lives, I can face tomorrow
Because He lives, all fear is gone
Because I know He holds the future
And life is worth the living, just because He lives
And then one day, I'll cross the river
I'll fight life's final war with pain
And then, as death gives way to victory
I'll see the lights of glory and I'll know He reigns
Because He lives, I can face tomorrow
Because He lives, all fear is gone
Because I know He holds the future
And life is worth the living, just because He lives
I can face tomorrow
Because He lives, all fear is gone
Because I know He holds the future
And life is worth the liv-
ing, just because He lives.[9]

And the song that I live with and love best is "Where No One Stands Alone." I feel sure that you have your list too or that you can develop one. Yes, I love beautiful music. Someone said, "If I can control the music of the world, I can control the world."

Where No One Stands Alone

By Thomas Mosie Lister

Once I stood in the night with
my head bowed low
In the darkness, as black as could be
And my heart felt alone
And I cried oh Lord
Don't hide your face from me
Hold my hand all the way
Every hour every day
From here to the grave
I know
Take my hand
Let me stand
Where no one stands alone
Like a king I may live in a palace so tall
With great riches to call my own
But I don't know a thing
In this whole wide world
That's worse than being alone
Hold me hand all the way
Every hour, every day
From here to the grave
I know
Take my hand
Let me stand
Where no one stands alone
Take my hand

Let me stand
Where no one stands alone[10]

The Transforming Power of Prayer

Now, I would like to bring up the subject of prayer again. Some years ago, I did some research for a speech. I gathered some interpretive statements concerning prayer from people who are servants of the Father and who live by the Father's teachings. Through this exasperating illness, I have often referred to their responses. I have greatly benefitted from their teaching, and I know that you will also.

M. Norvel Young said, "Through prayer, I have found God's strength in my weakness; His sufficiency in my lack. We kneel how weak, we rise again, how strong. I feel like a child wading in the shallows of the ocean and out there far beyond is infinitely more when I think of resources for the Christian in prayer and how much we need to launch out into the deep."

Batsell Barrett Baxter said (as he was in the last stages of cancer), "I have learned not to pray for recovery, though I have wanted to live for my family and my work's sake, but rather to pray, 'Thy Will Be Done.'"

Ruel Lemmons said, "As a pair of pliers in the hands of a man increases his grip, so prayer brings to our limited powers the illimitable resources of God."

Ira North said, "I have found that it is almost uncanny at how you can come up with the right decision when you spend some time in private and quiet, alone and in prayer."

Ruth Collins said, "I cannot imagine the great void that must be in the lives of those who cannot and will not turn to God for their strength."

Margie Overton wrote, "I have often wondered how a person who doesn't pray could possibly bear all his burdens. I am so thankful that I can take my burdens to the Lord and leave them there. I can with full assurance say that God will give us the strength of body and mind to face each day's problems. When my son, Timothy died, I learned more fully the meaning of prayer. I could not have born the deep sorrow I felt, (and still feel) if I did not believe that God hears and answers prayer. I thank God for prayer."

These statements are not all that I have received, but enough, I think, to let you know how much they mean to me. Read what Paul the apostle said:

> And pray in the Spirit on all occasions with all kinds of prayers and requests. With this in mind, be alert and always keep on praying for all the Lord's people. (Ephesians 6:18)

> Be joyful in hope, patient in affliction, faithful in prayer. (Romans 12:12)

> Devote yourselves to prayer, being watchful and thankful. (Colossians 4:2)

I could write scriptures on and on that show God's promise and power in prayer.

If your life of pain is not aimed toward the direction that it should be aimed, start praying in faith, and it just may change your aim. Prayer has played and is playing a significant role in my life. Often, as I cried, pleaded, and urged God to give me relief just for a moment, I would think, *What do people do in situations like this when they don't believe in him?* The worst feeling that I could imagine is not having an all-powerful God to call upon. How dreadful!

Many times, the nurses and doctors would seem inadequate in their knowledge, or they didn't have the proper tools needed to care for me, or sometimes it seemed that they were deaf and dumb to me. At times, I had the feeling that no one really cared about me.

Realization is a burden-lifting experience to know that God is always tuned in to me, and I take great comfort in the fact that, oh yes, he cares!

When one realizes that God understands and will help him, it brings relief to know that he is close enough to hear my voice.

Having an open dialogue with the Father is more than amazing! When ill health comes our way, the foundation of our soul will hold firm, because God said that he will never forsake us. I feel that He is with me even unto the end of the world.

David said in the twenty-third psalm (KJV), "Yea, though I walk through the valley of death." (Or pain, he is there!)

No medication, therapy, or counsel will take the place of God in suffering, ever. There is a popular song entitled "Lean on Me." That is what God is saying to us. Yes, God wants us to talk to him. He knows our needs, and he takes care of us whether or not we ask, but with his pleading for my attention and my pleading for his attention, I know that action is going to happen in heaven's realm. The mountains of life start trembling and moving, and our mental stress begins to ease.

In our worship services, we are learning a new song entitled "Our God Is an Awesome God." This title says it all. He is! Man often waffles or hedges, but God doesn't. He is the same yesterday, today, and tomorrow. I hope that my prayers are a sweet savor unto the Lord!

Gleaning Chapter 5 for Training in Love

1. What is the situation or problem? Helping the patient to heal through music and prayer.
2. Why does it matter? Because it has been proven to help comfort those who are suffering.
3. How do you engage in healthy conversations about it?

The Gifts of Art and Music

While we've come to think of the arts as a form of entertainment and even as personal expression, many of us have long forgotten that the arts also offer us opportunities to heal. In the distant past, the purpose of Greek drama was to produce an emotional catharsis. Tibetan monks still use chanting, bells, and "singing bowls" as part of their prayer and healing, and many native cultures include drumming, song, and dance as part of their ritual.

The joy you feel when creating art can be healing. It's easy to get "lost" in your creativity, relieving stress and thereby eliminating a major cause of disease. But the effects are even more profound. According to the Art as a Healing Force website (www.artashealing. org), scientific studies have shown that art literally changes not only a person's attitude but also their physiology. Art and music affect a person's brain wave pattern, along with the autonomic nervous system, hormonal balance, brain neurotransmitters, immune system, and blood flow to all the organs. They change one's perceptions of the world, including their emotional state and perception of pain.

The body is made to heal itself, and it heals best when in a state of deep relaxation. Art and music can bring the body into its natural state of balance and harmony so it can best do what it was meant to do. Many of us, when creating, become so absorbed that we fall naturally into that "altered" state. Scientists with highly sensitive measuring devices have discovered that, when we are in deep meditation or relaxation, the frequency of our electromagnetic field becomes attuned to that of the earth—a state of harmony. Composers such as Stephen Halpern (www.innerpeacemusic.com) specialize in creating music that assists the body in aligning to this frequency.

The arts have found their way into modern medicine as well. Surgeon and author Bernie Siegel has used drawing as a diagnostic tool in determining the optimal treatment for his patients. The University of Florida/Shands HealthCare (along with the medical facilities at Dartmouth, Stanford, and others) has incorporated an arts in medicine program (www.shands.org/aim/). Their mission is to bring together patients and caregivers—both staff and family members—to explore their creative energy through such forms as music, dance, singing, painting, drawing, writing, clowning, puppetry and magic. This empowers patients to strengthen their own inherent resources and do their own healing by regenerating body, mind, and spirit.[11]

Adult coloring books and coloring pencils are very popular right now. You can pick them up at your favorite grocery or drugstore. They make a nice gift for your patient.

The Transforming Power of Prayer

> Just as God transforms the hearts of young men through prayer, prayer can be the tool to transform communities and the leadership and direction of nations.
>
> The need for prayer and the divine guidance, protection and benefit that prayer provides is as needed today as it has ever been. I believe that prayer changes the hearts and minds of people who are prayed for, that prayer changes the circumstances for the impoverished and downtrodden, and that prayer changes the strength of those who intercede in prayer for others. Just as much, I believe we grow closer to God as we pray. I also believe we grow closer to those for whom we pray, and we grow closer to those with whom we pray. (Ben Carson)[12]

Lord, Teach Us to Pray (Luke 11:1)

Some people have a gift of being able to pray anytime with anyone about anything. Others find it more difficult to speak out loud the deepest desires of their heart, whether for themselves or others.

For Discussion

1. As an exercise in learning to pray, find a quiet time to write a generic prayer to carry with you for those occasions you want to pray out loud with or for someone in distress. Write it as though you were in the presence of that special person, and call them by name. Then talk to God on their behalf.
2. Discuss with one another some techniques you can use to make praying for someone more personal.

3.

4.

5.

CHAPTER 6

The Road from 2007

Change is in the air. The apples are getting ripe. Hunters are getting ready for dove season. The leaves are beginning to change. The nightly temperatures have already been in the low sixties. The farmers are harvesting the crops they have left after the drought. School is back in session. The Atlanta Braves have just swept the San Francisco Giants in a series, trying to catch them to be in the playoffs. A new quarter is beginning at church. There are so may pictures that I want to paint. People are being baptized. Many families are coming to worship and serve with us. The '96 Olympics are coming to Atlanta.

I cannot worry about tomorrow; it is going to happen. All I have is today. I want to make sure I can strengthen the physical abilities that I have left. That means that I am constantly developing goals that keep me active.

I will be going to the Emory Spinal Center for therapy shortly, and hopefully, the pain will somehow be less today.

In my life now, I must let God talk to me often through his Word.

I must talk to my Father in heaven several times a day.

I must see at least four different doctors a month.

I must listen to beautiful music and singing.

I must go to physical therapy continuously and give in to the idea "I won't go today."

I must read the best books and literature.

73

I must constantly remind myself that God did not have a slipup when he came to me.

I must constantly see about people that are in awesome un-get-over-able circumstance.

I must take all my medicine every day.

I must learn to accept the things that I cannot change.

I must make myself accessible to other people for my own mental salvation.

I must always know that this world is not and never will be my home.

I must always be myself.

I must realize that pain is not fatal.

I must understand that it was not my fault when I had the accident.

I must not live with the words "if only" in my heart.

There is, I believe, a silver lining in each cloud. I just need to bring it into focus.

It has been very helpful for me to write this book over the past two years. Maybe it would be helpful for you to do the same, just to get something off your heart and out of your mind. If you cannot type or write, you may consider dictating your life into a tape recorder. Your special story needs to be told so people around you can learn.

I must remember my true saying: "If life were any other way, it would be different." Let me encourage you to remember it too.

Will you agree with me that "this moment is the only moment that we have"?

We are not promised another one. Let us not waste it in self-pity!

I think that I want to end this book with two statements: "*We must endure*" and "*For me to live is Christ, and to die is gain*" (Philippians 1:21).

Gleaning Chapter 6 for Training in Love

1. What is the situation or problem? Patient attitude adjustments and cooperation with your home team are badly needed.

2. Why does it matter? Patients need to realize that it's easier when you love yourself and try to take care of yourself.
3. How do you engage in healthy conversations about it?

Editor's note: Since David's book was first published, there has been more research about living with chronic pain and depression. The internet is a resource for valuable information. For those who live with pain and for those who want to help those who live with pain, these tips are worthy of consideration.

Living with Chronic Pain—11 Tips from the Internet[13]

1. Learn deep breathing or meditation to help you relax.
2. Reduce stress in your life. Stress intensifies chronic pain.
3. Boost chronic pain relief with the natural endorphins from exercise.
4. Cut back on alcohol, which can worsen sleep problems.
5. Join a support group. Meet others living with chronic pain.
6. Don't smoke. It can worsen chronic pain.
7. Track your pain level and activities every day.
8. Learn biofeedback to decrease migraine and tension headache pain.
9. Get a massage for chronic pain relief.
10. Eat a healthy diet if you're living with chronic pain.
11. Find ways to distract yourself from pain so you enjoy life more.
12. Read the entire article at http://www.webmd.com/pain-management/guide/11-tips-for-living-with-chronic-pain#1

Remember the Caregiver

Last, but not least, pay attention to Carolyn's advice, and remember the caregiver!

Praise be to the God and Father of our Lord Jesus Christ, the Father of compassion and the God of all comfort. (2 Corinthians 1:3)

For Discussion

Make a list of things that can be done for the Caregiver that will be helpful and encouraging. How can your hands be the hands of Jesus in these circumstances?

1)

2)

3.

4)

5)

CHAPTER 7

Seeing the Holy Spirit and Walking Around the Borders of Misunderstanding through the Gates of Grace

Year 2017—since writing my book, *A Cry for Relief*, I have been in numerous painful situations where I thought "Oh, God, can you hear me?" concerning the Holy Spirit and grace in my daily life. My quest has become to look again at the God who made me and the God who saved me and the Spirit who brought the power of salvation to mankind. As my life has progressed over these number of years, I have a lot of flashbacks to biblical topics, which, had I only looked into them and known more about the truth of them at the time of my injury, would have been of immense value to me while trying to deal with my pain and agony.

Subjects such as grace and the Holy Spirit working in my everyday walk of life, and not only through the Bible, are subjects that I have been studying much more in the past several years. I have sat at the feet of learned men who have done exhaustive studies on their own.

The Holy Spirit Intercedes for God's People

When we were baptized, we were all made to drink of the one Spirit (1 Corinthians 12–13), so then what? Did he leave us then?

Notice in the passages below, there are direct statements that describe our partnership with the Spirit. We have the option of enhancing the impact of the Spirit in our lives. Paul refers to this as keeping in step with the Spirit. It appears as though there is a direct connection between our being in step with the Spirit and the "full-blooming" fruits of the Spirit. The Word of God is very clear in these matters. This has helped me to understand the place and Word of the Spirit and grace in my thoughts. Understanding these things is a great benefit for me. However, if you have never suffered dramatically, it may be hard to grasp these thoughts.

Romans 8:12–18, 26–28:

> Therefore, brothers and sisters, we have an obligation—but it is not to the flesh, to live according to it. For if you live according to the flesh, you will die; but if by the Spirit you put to death the misdeeds of the body, you will live. For those who are led by the Spirit of God are the children of God. The Spirit you received does not make you slaves, so that you live in fear again; rather, the Spirit you received brought about your adoption to son ship. And by him we cry, "Abba, Father."
>
> The Spirit himself testifies with our spirit that we are God's children. Now if we are children, then we are heirs—heirs of God and co-heirs with Christ, if indeed we share in his sufferings in order that we may also share in his glory. I consider that our present sufferings are not worth comparing with the glory that will be revealed in us.

In the same way, the Spirit helps us in our weakness. We do not know what we ought to pray for, but the Spirit himself intercedes for us through wordless groans. And he who searches our hearts knows the mind of the Spirit, because the Spirit intercedes for God's people in accordance with the will of God.

And we know that in all things God works for the good of those who love him, who have been called according to his purpose.

1 Corinthians 2:9–16:

However, as it is written:

"*What no eye has seen, what no ear has heard, and what no human mind has conceived*"—the things God has prepared for those who love him—these are the things God has revealed to us by his Spirit.

The Spirit searches all things, even the deep things of God. For who knows a person's thoughts except their own spirit within them? In the same way no one knows the thoughts of God except the Spirit of God. What we have received is not the spirit of the world, but the Spirit who is from God, so that we may understand what God has freely given us. This is what we speak, not in words taught us by human wisdom but in words taught by the Spirit, explaining spiritual realities with Spirit- taught words. The person without the Spirit does not accept the things that come from the Spirit of God but considers them foolishness, and cannot understand them because they are discerned only through the Spirit. The person with the Spirit makes judgments about all things, but such a person is not subject to merely human judgments, for,

"Who has known the mind of the Lord so as to instruct him? But we have the mind of Christ."

Galatians 5:16, 17:

So I say, walk by the Spirit, and you will not gratify the desires of the flesh. For the flesh desires what is contrary to the Spirit, and the Spirit what is contrary to the flesh. They are in conflict with each other, so that you are not to do whatever you want. But if you are led by the Spirit, you are not under the law.

Titus 3:5:

But when the kindness and love of God our Savior appeared, he saved us, not because of righteous things we had done, but because of his mercy. He saved us through the washing of rebirth and renewal by the Holy Spirit.

Grace

Grace is a subject that was not emphasized in the early years of my Bible study, in my fellowship, or in my personal life. Over the years, as I have grown in my faith and understanding of his word, I have come to understand and appreciate God's grace more clearly. For much of my Christian life, I focused more on his wrath and justice. I saw him more as a courtroom God looking for justice. Knowing my human condition, this made me afraid; relating to him fearfully rather than lovingly.

Over the past three decades, my health issues have exposed me to him in ways that made me look for him and seek him in ways

I had not previously experienced. As I cried out to him for relief I found what was missing in my theology. I discovered his marvelous grace and that he is not the courtroom God who is trying to find a way to condemn me. I discovered that he really does care and that he understands me better than I understand myself. I discovered that he is the great redeemer and loves me so much he gave his son for my sins. I believe and accept the blessed assurance that he promises as an expression of his grace and mercy.

First John 1:7 reassures me that the blood of Christ cleanses me from all my sin.

> But if we walk in the light, as he is in the light, we have fellowship with one another, and the blood of Jesus, his Son, *purifies us from all sin.*

The grace of God is not only a New Testament subject. God extended his grace throughout the Old Testament.

> But Noah found grace in the eyes of the LORD. (Genesis 6:8)

God spared Lot and his family.

> Your servant has found favor (grace) in your eyes, and you have shown great kindness to me in sparing my life. But I can't flee to the mountains; this disaster will overtake me, and I'll die. Look, here is a town near enough to run to, and it is small. Let me flee to it—it is very small, isn't it? Then my life will be spared.

You must understand that I wondered why the God of love would keep allowing me to be punished over and over, again and again. A dear friend of mine once asked me, "David, what in the world have you done to make God hate you this much?" That is really the way I felt. But time and additional reliance on God and his Word have taught me to think differently.

His Grace Reaches Me

Music and Lyrics: Jewell M.
Whitey Gleason, 1964

Deeper than the ocean and wider than the sea,
Is the grace of the Savior for sinners like me;
Sent from the Father and it thrills my soul,
Just to feel and to know
That His blood makes me whole.
Higher than the mountains and
brighter than the sun,
It was offered at Calvary for everyone;
Greatest of treasures and it's mine today,
Though my sins were as scarlet,
He has washed them away.

Chorus:

His grace reaches me
And 'twill last thru eternity;
Now I'm under His control
And I'm happy in my soul,
Just to know that His grace reaches me.[14]

Ephesians 2:4–10:

"But because of his great love for us, God, who is rich in mercy, made us alive with Christ even when we were dead in transgressions—it is by grace you have been saved. And God raised us up with Christ and seated us with him in the heavenly realms in Christ Jesus, in order that in the coming ages he might show the incomparable riches of his grace, expressed in his kindness to us in Christ Jesus. For it is by grace you have been saved, through faith—and this is not from yourselves, it is the gift of God—not by works, so that no one can boast. For we are God's handiwork, created in Christ Jesus to do good works, which God prepared in advance for us to do.

Ephesians 3:7, 8:

I became a servant of this gospel by the gift of God's grace given me through the working of his power. Although I am less than the least of all the Lord's people, this grace was given me: to preach to the Gentiles the boundless riches of Christ.

2 Timothy 1:9:

He has saved us and called us to a holy life—not because of anything we have done but because of his own purpose and grace. This grace was given us in Christ Jesus before the beginning of time.

Titus 3:5:

But when the kindness and love of God our Savior appeared, he saved us, not because of righteous things we had done, but because of his mercy. He saved us through the washing of rebirth and renewal by the Holy Spirit.

James 2:20–24:

You foolish person, do you want evidence that faith without deeds is useless? Was not our father Abraham considered righteous for what he did when he offered his son Isaac on the altar? You see that his faith and his actions were working together, and his faith was made complete by what he did. And the scripture was fulfilled that says, "Abraham believed God, and it was credited to him as righteousness," and he was called God's friend. You see that a person is considered righteous by what they do and not by faith alone.

My wife and I have had as many of the same insurmountable problems as other people have had. If I told you, in full disclosure, you would not believe how much could happen to one Christian couple. Time after time, we have been driven to our knees with no earthly help in sight, but God came through. We have been blessed with grace and favor time and time again.

God, Christ, the Holy Spirit, and the heavenly host are waiting for your call. Thank you for making time to read my book. My prayer is that it will be a blessing to you to have read it, as it was for me to have written it.

Gleaning Chapter 7 for Training in Love

1. What is the situation or problem? Helping the patient to recognize the Holy Spirit and grace in everyday life.
2. Why does it matter? A daily dose of the holy scriptures is very encouraging.
3. How do you engage in healthy conversations about it?

Grace: More Than We Deserve, Greater Than We Imagine: An Interview with Max Lucado[15]

Max Lucado explains why we must embrace the whole truth about grace.

Q: What better way to start than with your definition of grace?

A: To put it very simply, grace is God's best idea—it's his decision to ravage a people by love, to rescue passionately, and to restore justly.

Q: This isn't the first time you've written about grace. What makes this book different from all that's already been printed?

A: Most books on the topic—including ones I've written—focus on what grace is. While this book covers that, its focus is on what grace *does*. How grace changes us. And I'm not just talking about what it means for us in terms of being forgiven and going to heaven, but also what it means for the changes in our hearts and attitudes. Grace is the voice that calls us to change, and then gives us the power to pull it off. Most books on grace miss the "power to pull it off" part. And that's the heart of this book.

Q: How does the concept of grace make Christianity different from other world religions?

A: When grace happens, we receive not a nice compliment from God but a new heart. Give your heart to Christ, and he returns the favor. "I will give you a new heart and put a new spirit within you" (Ezekiel 36:26). For many years I missed this truth. I believed all the other prepositions: Christ for me, with me, ahead of me. And I knew I was working beside Christ, under Christ, with Christ. But I never imagined that Christ was in me. No other religion or philosophy makes such a claim. No other movement implies the living presence of its founder in his followers. Muhammad does not indwell Muslims. Buddha does not inhabit Buddhists. The Christian is a person in whom Christ is happening.

Q: You describe grace as God aggressively moving toward us.

A: Yes. Rather than tell us to change, he creates the change. Do we clean up so he can accept us? No, he accepts us and begins cleaning us up. Grace is God as heart surgeon, cracking open your chest, removing your heart—poisoned as it is with pride and pain—and replacing it with his own. His dream isn't just to get you into heaven but to get heaven into you.

Q: You say grace brings rest. Why is this not the case for many believers?

A: We find it easier to trust the miracle of resurrection than the miracle of grace. We so fear failure that we create the image of perfection, lest heaven be even more disappointed in us than we are. The result? The weariest people on earth. Attempts at self-salvation guarantee nothing but exhaustion. We scamper and scurry, trying to please God, collecting merit badges and brownie points, and scowling at anyone who questions our accomplishments. Call us the church of hound-dog faces and slumped shoulders. God's promise has no hidden language. Let grace happen, for heaven's sake. No more performance for God, no more clamoring after God. Of all the things you must earn in life, God's unending affection is not one of them. You have it. Stretch yourself out in the hammock of grace. You can rest now.

Q: What's the difference between grace and mercy?

A: Grace goes beyond mercy. Mercy gave the prodigal son a second chance. Grace threw him a party. Mercy prompted the Samaritan to bandage the wounds of the victim. Grace prompted him to leave his credit card as payment for the victim's care. Mercy forgave the thief on the cross. Grace escorted him into paradise. Mercy pardons us. Grace woos and weds us.

Q: The concept of saving grace is familiar to many people. What do you mean when you write about sustaining grace?

A: Saving grace saves us from our sins. Sustaining grace meets us at our point of need and equips us with courage, wisdom, and strength. It surprises us in the middle of our difficulties with ample resources of faith. Sustaining grace does not promise the absence of struggle but the presence of God. And according to Paul, God has sufficient sustaining grace to meet every single challenge of our lives. Sufficient. *Grace* is simply another word for his tumbling, rumbling reservoir of strength and protection. It comes at us not occasionally or miserly but constantly and aggressively, wave upon wave. We've barely regained our balance from one breaker, and then, bam, here comes another. God's grace dethrones your fears. Anxiety still comes, for certain. The globe still heats up; wars still flare up; the economy acts up. Disease, calamity, and trouble populate your world. But they don't control it! Grace does.

Q: You say that grace is God's answer to the question everyone asks: *Do I matter?* which ultimately sounds like a question of identity.

A: Absolutely. We validate our existence with a flurry of activity. We do more, buy more, and achieve more. Like Jacob, we wrestle. All our wrestlings, I suppose, are merely asking this question: "Do I matter?" All of grace, I believe, is God's definitive reply: "Be blessed, my child. I accept you. I have adopted you into my family." Adopted children are chosen children. To accept God's grace is to accept God's offer to be adopted into his family. Your identity is not in your possessions, talents, tattoos, kudos, or accomplishments. Nor are you defined by your divorce, deformity, debt, or dumb choices. You are God's child. You get to call him "Papa." You "may approach God with freedom and confidence" (Ephesians 3:12). You receive the blessings of his special love (1 John 4:9-11) and provision (Luke 11:11-13). And you will inherit the riches of Christ and reign with him forever (Romans 8:17).

Q: As a result of this powerful grace, we can trust God's love for us is unending care.

A: Yes, which means that rather than conjure up reasons to feel good about yourself, trust God's verdict. If God loves you, you must be worth loving. If he wants to have you in his kingdom, then you must be worth having. God's grace invites you—no, *requires* you—to change your attitude about yourself and take sides with God against your feelings of rejection. To live as God's child is to know, at this very instant, that you are loved by your Maker not because you try to please him and succeed, or fail to please him and apologize, but because he wants to be your Father. Nothing more. All your efforts to win his affection are unnecessary. All your fears of losing his affection are needless. You can no more make him want you than you can convince him to abandon you. The adoption is irreversible. You have a place at his table.[16]

For Discussion

In groups of four or more, discuss how you think the concept of grace helps those who are in pain and suffering.

1.

2.

3.

4.

5.

APPENDIX A

A Perspective from David's Wife, Carolyn, the Caregiver

I must be the first to admit that I am not a writer or public speaker. I have always been uncomfortable when placed in a spotlight position. Unlike David, who, for many years, was a minister and had always loved people and being involved in their lives. I guess this is why it has taken me so long to accept his disability.

I have been asked by several friends to write a chapter for the book and tell how I have coped, in the hope of offering some help to those who find themselves in similar circumstances.

The last five years have found me questioning many things about me as a person and my faith in God. I have gone through most of the normal disappointments in life in rearing three children, losing both parents and my in-laws, but nothing has been as hard as seeing my husband lose his health.

Many may say I have so much to be thankful for and there are so many people with greater problems. This is true, but you are unable to see those blessings at the time. You find out firsthand that there is a vast difference in talking the game of life and playing the game of life.

After the failed surgery in March 1990, my faith became so very weak. For the first time, I was very angry when I finally faced the truth that David was much worse and would not be able to return to a normal life we had known. After all, we were both in our prime!

Had it not been for Jesse Long at Greater Atlanta Christian School, where David was employed when the injury occurred, and many of our friends, we would have been in great financial difficulty.

Now that you have heard my negative side, let me share with you some of my feelings today. I still do not have answers to many questions, but I can tell you that, through your sad experiences, you can find solutions to your problems if you don't give in or give up.

Listed below are a few suggestions if you are faced with personal tragedy in your life:

1. Don't feel that life has been especially cruel to you, that is, singled you out; God is in control.
2. Don't feel guilty when your faith becomes weak. Only time can heal disappointment and hurt. Then you can emerge with a greater faith.
3. When faced with a mountain, don't quit. Learn to take one day at a time.
4. Learn to trust in God that he will take care of you. You cannot trust in your own financial planning.

Also, some suggestions or ways you may be of help to others who are caregivers:

1. Observe them, and express to them your interest in their well-being. Ask them how they are doing. I have, on several occasions, wanted to say, "Can't you see I am not doing well?"
2. Make conversation about other things besides the patient and how he is doing. A wise caregiver has told the same story repeatedly. In the case of a long-term illness or disability, there is usually not much change.
3. Never say "You are going to be a better person when this is over" or "God has a special plan for you when this is over." They may or may not be a better person. Even if they are, it is a truth they may not be able to fathom or appreciate at that time. (And what a price to pay for becoming a bet-

ter person, and why should God punish your loved one to make a better person of you?)

4. Don't forget the caregiver. We usually forget and move on, but they still need encouragement.

I must say how blessed our family has been. Christians from several states have been involved in our lives and have shown much concern and support. I cannot imagine life without family and friends in time of joy or sorrow. None of us know what the future holds, and I am thankful that God has not allowed any of us to see into it. But we can know that sunshine follows the rain and joy cometh in the morning.

APPENDIX B

David's Additional Thoughts on Depression

With a complex illness or injury, it is very hard just trying to relay your pain and agony to someone else. There is help if we but call upon God, Christ, and the Holy Spirit. But it is easy to forget that they may show up as the arms of friends.

These feelings of loss and grief can recur many times during the journey of healing:

- When I stand on the seashore and watch a big and beautiful ocean liner set sail then go out of sight. I think, *I wish I were on that ship.*
- I watch the superlarge air liners take off and think, *I wish I were going.*
- I try to muster the strength to blot these things, these losses, out of my mind, but I cannot.
- All I can think about is my ship has sailed or my planes have left me at the gate.
- I think, I am really a loser, destressed, depressed, and I just want to hide away in a faraway place.
- I think, I care not for my soul. It is hard to get people to empathize.

Reading this, you may not understand, but please try. You can make a big difference.

APPENDIX C

Suggested Readings

1. *If God Is Good: Faith in the Midst of Suffering and Evil*, by Randy Alcorn
2. *Finding the Heart to Go On*, by Lynn Anderson
3. *When God Doesn't Make Sense*, by Dr. James Dobson
4. *You Gotta Keep Dancin'*, by Tim Hansel
5. *Walking with God through Pain and Suffering*, by Timothy Keller
6. *When Bad Things Happen to Good People*, by Harold S. Kushner
7. *God Came Near*, by Max Lucado
8. *Grace: More Than We Deserve, Greater Than We Imagine*, by Max Lucado
9. *You'll Get Through This: Hope and Help for Your Turbulent Times*, by Max Lucado
10. *Through the Eyes of a Lion: Facing Impossible Pain, Finding Incredible Power*, by Levi Lusko (author), Steven Furtick (foreword)
11. *Happiness Is a Choice*, by Frank B. Minirth, MD, and Paul D. Meier, MD
12. *A Long Obedience in the Same Direction*, by Eugene H. Peterson
13. *Reversed Thunder*, by Eugene H. Peterson
14. *Healing Grace*, by David A. Seamands

15. *The Hallelujah Factor,* by Jack R. Taylor
16. *Think,* by Virgil R. Trout
17. *Disappointment with God,* by Philip Yancey
18. *A Grace Disguised: How the Soul Grows through Loss,* by Jerry L. Sittser

Endnotes

1. "Walking with God through Pain and Suffering, Timothy Keller, Copyright © 2013

2. *Merriam-Webster Dictionary* definition of *glean*:
intransitive verb
1: to gather grain or other produce left by reapers
2: to gather information or material bit by bit
transitive verb
1a: to pick up after a reaper b: to strip (as a field) of the leavings of reapers
2a: to gather (as information) bit by bit <can *glean* secrets from his hard drive> b: to pick over in search of relevant material <*gleaning* old files for information>

3. Ronald K. Rittgers, *The Reformation of Suffering: Pastoral Theology and Lay Piety in Late Medieval and Early Modern Germany*, (Oxford Studies in Historical Theology.) 2012

4. Bible Verses to Comfort You - http://www.biblestudytools.com/topical-verses/bible-verses-to-comfort- you

5. By Blake Flannery https://holidappy.com/greeting-cards/ Encouraging-Messages-and-Quotes-Words-of-Encouragement

6. By Barrie Davenport, http://liveboldandbloom.com/07/ quotes/words-of-encouragement

7. https://www.merriam-webster.com/dictionary/tact

8. Written by Andrew Shawn Craig, Donald A. Koch. Copyright Universal Music Publishing Group, Capitol Christian Music Group.

9. Songwriters: Gloria Gaither and William J. Gaither. "Because He Lives" lyrics. Capitol Christian Music Group.

10. Songwriter: Thomas Mosie Lister. "Where No One Stands Alone" lyrics. Music Services Inc.

11. http://www.goodlifecoaching.com/CreativeLife16.html, by Sharon Good, BCC, ACC, CLC

12. http://www.washingtontimes.com/specials/power-prayer/

13. http://www.webmd.com/pain-management/guide/11-tips-for-living-with-chronic-pain#1

14. "His Grace Reaches Me." Music and lyrics: Jewell M. Whitey Gleason, 1964

15. http://www.christianitytoday.com/biblestudies/articles/spiritualformation/grace-more-than-we-deserve-greater-than-we-imagine.html?start=2

16. Copyright 2018, David A. Wheeler and Christianity Today/ChristianBibleStudies.com. Used with permission.

About the Author

David Wheeler was born in Bremen, Georgia. He is the youngest of eight children. He attended Faulkner University and Amridge University in Montgomery, Alabama.

David is a retired pulpit minister who lives with his wife, Carolyn, in Cumming, Georgia. They have been married for sixty years. He has served churches in Jacksonville, Florida; Lake Butler, Florida; Mobile, Alabama; East Tallassee, Alabama; and Charlotte, North Carolina. He also worked with Faulkner University in Montgomery, Alabama, and Greater Atlanta Christian School in Atlanta, Georgia.

David is a true gentleman who enjoys watercolor painting and likes to talk about his three children, six grandchildren, and three great-grandchildren.

David says, "My wife, Carolyn, is still my source of strength and love. Her love, encouragement, and constant care continue to make my life worth living. I am very thankful for her and my entire family, whose love and support give me hope for our future generations."

For the past thirty years, David has lived with physical pain as the result of a back injury and failed back surgeries. *A Cry for Relief* is an account of God working through the physical and emotional suffering of a person's life and helping him to discover the meaning of true joy on his journey.

Photo Courtesy Adrian Freeman Photography

CPSIA information can be obtained
at www.ICGtesting.com
Printed in the USA
FFOW02n0406040718
47275088-50194FF